DATE DUE

Demco No. 62-0549

METROPOLITAN COLLEGE
OF NEW YORK LIBRARY
75 Varick Street 12th Fl.
New York, NY 10013

CAREERS INSIDE THE WORLD OF
Environmental Science

Many people are working to clean up our environment.

CAREERS & OPPORTUNITIES

CAREERS INSIDE THE WORLD OF
Environmental Science

GE
60
G37
1995

by Robert Gartner

THE ROSEN PUBLISHING GROUP, INC.
NEW YORK

For Amy

Published in 1995 by The Rosen Publishing Group, Inc.
29 East 21st Street, New York, NY 10010

Copyright 1995 by The Rosen Publishing Group, Inc.

All rights reserved. No part of this book may be reproduced in any form without permission in writing from the publisher, except by a reviewer.

First Edition

Manufactured in the United States of America

Library of Congress Cataloging-in-Publication Data

Gartner, Robert.
    Careers inside the world of environmental science / by Bob Gartner.—1st ed.
       p.   cm.—(Careers & opportunities)
    Includes bibliographical references and index.
    ISBN 0-8239-1903-X
1. Environmental sciences—Vocational guidance—Juvenile literature.
[1. Environmental sciences—Vocational guidance. 2. Vocational guidance. 3. Occupations.] I. Title. II. Series.
GE60.G37   1995
363.7'0023 — dc20   94-19046
                                                                                 CIP
                                                                                     AC

Contents

    Introduction 6
1. Environmental Connections 9
2. Is This Career for You? 12
3. Environmental Careers 16
4. Gaining Experience 39
5. Getting the Job 46
6. Career Tips 54
    Glossary 58
    Appendix 60
    For Further Reading 62
    Index 63

INTRODUCTION

Even before the First Earth Day in 1970, the environment was a major concern of the American public. Environmental activism spread around the world. Citizens took their concern to their countries' leaders. More people started to take individual action to save the environment.

Inspired by the people, the United States Congress passed environmental laws. The Environmental Protection Agency was created to enforce those laws. With all this attention to the environment, many businesses had to change the way they operated. Polluting companies were obliged to obey the laws to limit their air and water pollutants.

New businesses and technologies developed to control pollution and recycle solid waste. New job opportunities were created. People became interested in environmental careers. If you are interested in making the earth a safer place for everyone, this book will introduce you to the different kinds of environmental careers.

Americans have been especially concerned about the health and safety of the environment for the last three decades.

Many cities and towns have celebrations for a greener earth.

CHAPTER 1

ENVIRONMENTAL CONNECTIONS

Amy was excited as she picked up Julia on Saturday. They were driving to the County Conservation Fair. The Fair was an annual event featuring displays by conservation groups, businesses, and government agencies. Each display showed what that organization was doing to improve the environment.

Admission to the Fair was one bag of recyclable materials. Amy had brought a bag of plastic bottles, and Julia had a box of old newspapers. Inside the Fair, the booths displayed brochures and magazines describing the various organizations. Some booths had ongoing videos or slide shows.

There were some groups at the Fair promoting recycling. Other groups were involved in protection of endangered species such as whales. People were soliciting signatures on petitions to Congress to strengthen the Clean Air and Clean Water Acts. They had sign-up sheets for volunteers. The county sanitary landfill and wastewater treatment plant had displays. The National Wildlife Federation had a large booth filled with beautiful photographs of wildlife and birds. A poster featured the wings of butterflies from all over the world. The colorful design on each wing displayed a letter of the alphabet from a to z.

One Circle

A large circular booth caught Julia's eye. She waved for Amy to come over. The sign outside read "The Circle." Inside, the display featured photos and drawings that told a story. The pictures started near the door and moved to the right until you completed the circle. The first panel explained that the word "environment" come from the Old French word *viron*, which means circle. The display showed how everything on earth is connected and how every being on earth is affected by what is happening to the environment.

Every action starts a chain reaction. When a tree is cut down, more carbon dioxide remains in the air because trees remove carbon dioxide. Carbon dioxide is one of the main causes of global warming and air pollution. As temperatures rise, more water from rivers and lakes evaporates and the earth becomes drier. Soils are held together by the root systems of trees. Once the trees are removed, the soils lose their anchor and are eroded by winds. The eroded soils are swept into rivers. They settle onto the bottom and cover fish nesting beds, suffocating the fish eggs and the aquatic insects. Fewer fish are born, and the birds and animals that feed on the fish and insects move away in search of more food. These chain reactions go on and on.

"I had no idea that every action starts a chain reaction," said Julia.

"But Julia, everything we do to help the environment also starts a chain reaction. Only this time it is a series of helpful actions," responded Amy.

Because everything is connected, anything that you do to help the environment, personally and in your career, is a step toward saving the earth. This concern for the earth's environment leads people to seek careers that improve the earth.

Questions to Ask Yourself

Everything we do affects something else. Our actions create a circle linking humans and the earth. Think about how this happens. 1) What is a chain reaction? 2) How do chain reactions affect the earth? 3) What are some recyclable materials?

CHAPTER 2

IS THIS CAREER FOR YOU?

Before you read further, you should examine your feelings about the environment. How important to you is a career working to improve the environment? What do you do in your everyday life to help the earth? Could you be happy working at a job you enjoyed that didn't pay much?

You can't be effective in any work unless you care about it and consider it important. If improving the environment is a high priority with you, an environmental career may fit you to a T.

The expression "Walk the talk" applies to an environmental career. It means that you can't just talk about your concern for the environment: You have to back up your words with action. Do you recycle? Have you stopped using aerosol sprays that damage the ozone layer? Are you limiting your use of energy by turning out lights and walking short distances rather than driving? Are you part of a school or community group that is environmentally active? Examine how you live and what you personally are doing to help the environment. Decide whether or not you are "walking the talk." If you are, you should explore the careers described in this book.

You do not need a college degree to get a job in the environmental field. As in many careers, the more education you have, the better are your chances of landing a higher-paid position. Some positions require an advanced degree—a master's or a doctorate. Typically, these positions also pay better.

Generally, private industry pays the best, followed by the federal government. State governments come next, and then local governments (county, city, town). Traditionally, the lowest-paying positions are with the environmental organizations. Most of them depend on donations from their members and the public to fund their operations. They have to keep their costs down.

If you choose an environmental career that has a shortage of qualified people, you can expect to receive a higher salary. Engineers are always in demand, as are many people qualified in technical positions.

A career working to improve the environment provides a wonderful sense of satisfaction. Besides seeking to stop the destruction of the earth, many of the careers actually save people's lives. Jobs that improve the air and water directly affect people's health. Hazardous-waste specialists train workers to protect themselves from the dangerous materials they handle constantly. Environmental technicians test air, water, and soil samples. They notify the health authorities when pollution amounts are high enough to be dangerous to our health.

Few satisfactions can compare with saving someone's life. Park rangers, firemen, and policemen will tell you that saving a life is their greatest satisfaction. Workers in environmental careers feel a similar fulfillment because they are saving the earth and indirectly saving human lives.

As we saw in Chapter 1, all things are connected. When we improve one element of the environment, it starts a chain reaction that affects other elements. So no matter what you do in your environmental career, you are improving the overall health of the earth and its human and animal citizens.

Questions to Ask Yourself

Explore your own feelings about the environment. Not everyone is ready to make the commitment to a greener world. 1) Do you "walk the talk"? What do you do right now that helps the environment? 2) Why do you think it's important to help save the environment?

Forestry technicians fight forest fires.

CHAPTER 3

ENVIRONMENTAL CAREERS

There are many environmental positions available. Some require college degrees and some do not. We will cover both types of positions here.

Environmental Careers Without College
Jobs as technicians are available in almost every type of environmental work. The technician performs a wide variety of tasks, working under the supervision of a professional employee. Technical jobs do require training. Some require a two-year associate degree. In others, on-the-job training will teach you what you need to know. Let's look at some of the technician positions.

Natural Resource Management Technicians
Most of this work is done outdoors. The work includes fish and wildlife, forestry, parks and recreation, and land-use management.

Fish and wildlife technicians are constantly in the field. They may spend a day building nesting boxes for wood ducks or restocking a trout stream. Recently, technicians working for the U.S. Fish and Wildlife Service spent a day counting eagles at the Blackwater National Wildlife Refuge in southern Maryland. Thanks to the Endangered Species Act, which protects plants and animals that are in danger of extinction, American bald eagles are increasing in number. In 1972, there were only 400 pair of these eagles nationwide. During this count, the technicians spotted fifty nesting pairs in that refuge alone.

Technicians estimate fish populations by netting or shocking fish in a portion of a lake or stream. In Shenandoah National Park in Virginia, the fisheries biologist and three technicians electroshock the park's forty-two trout streams every summer. If a stream has a low population, it is closed to allow the trout to increase.

Fish and wildlife technicians take samples of the air and water to check for pollution. They also collect fish and animals to relocate them or to study diseases. In the national parks, bears that cause trouble are tranquilized and moved to remote areas rather than being destroyed.

The technicians also do habitat studies by evaluating small sample areas called transects. They mark the corners of a transect and count the numbers and varieties of plants within it. Are the plants native to the area or are they exotic (nonnative)? Is the soil eroded, compacted, or stable? Technicians record this information and present it to the resource manager. Together they examine the information and decide on the best way to protect or restore the area.

Forestry technicians also spend most of their time outdoors. One of their main duties is called "timber cruising." They go through the forest measuring the height and diameter of trees. With this information, they can estimate the amount, quality, and value of the lumber that would be produced by harvesting those trees. They also "thin" the forest by cutting down deformed or diseased trees. This allows the remaining trees to grow more rapidly.

Forestry technicians fight forest fires. This is a dangerous job. All firefighters receive special training. Working with forest engineers, they survey new road locations and survey property lines to prevent taking privately owned trees.

An important part of their job is ecosystem evaluation. While timber cruising, they also observe the wildlife and bird species in the area and the habitat. By knowing the habitat, they can predict what animals should be there. When endangered species live in the forest, the foresters can schedule their timber harvests to preserve the animals. On the coast of Washington State, bald eagles nest from January to June. The foresters

Working in a recycling plant helps clean up the environment directly.

schedule activities away from these sites during that time to avoid disturbing the eaglets.

When a forest harvest is planned, the technicians examine a map of the soils in the area and estimate the damage that will be done. They look for areas of soil erosion and compaction and decide how the activity of cutting and hauling trees will affect rivers or streams in the forest. If too much soil is washed into the water, the salmon and trout eggs will be covered and suffocated and the fish population will decline.

Once a harvest is under way, the technician is responsible for making sure that the logging company stays within the area of the cut. He or she preserves areas marked off-limits to protect wildlife, and protects the streams from soil runoff. After the area is logged, the technician may replant the area with new trees or oversee the contractor who comes in to do so.

A parks and recreation technician does work similar to that of the fish and wildlife technician. The parks and recreation technician also clears hiking trails, removes hazardous trees or tree limbs, leads nature walks, plants vegetation on hillsides to prevent erosion, and does general maintenance in the park.

Geology technicians work with a geologist. They do fieldwork such as collecting soil and rock samples from an area being studied as a dam site. From these samples the geologist determines whether the ground is strong enough to support the dam. Technicians also drill groundwater wells to test the chemical makeup of the water or test for pollutants. These groundwater tests are especially important if the water is near a landfill or hazardous-waste disposal site. The technician may test the ground-water weekly for years to ensure that it is not being polluted. Technicians work with scientific measuring instruments and learn to record and analyze the information they gather and to prepare field reports.

Land-use planning technicians work mainly with maps and aerial photographs. They spend a good amount of time in the field verifying information shown on the maps and photographs. This is known as "groundtruthing." Technicians gather information from satellite maps and use computers to plot land usage and draw maps to show trends in land use changes. With computers in almost every office, technicians today rarely use drafting tools. Instead, maps are made by using computer programs such as the geographic information system (GIS), which allows a large amount of geographic data to be shown.

Most of these jobs are with federal, state, and local governments, although private timber companies also hire forestry technicians.

Environmental Technicians
Wastewater treatment plant operators run and maintain the plant, which removes sewage and harmful chemicals and pollutants. The water is then clean enough to use again. Operators receive training in removing solids from the water, separating oil and water, and adjusting the chemicals needed to purify the water.

Sanitary landfill operator doesn't sound like a very glamorous job, but it is challenging and important. Garbage trucks bring in solid waste throughout the day, scatter their loads on the

Workers separate recyclables from other waste.

ground and go back for more. The solid waste is then covered with earth. The operator must make sure that the landfill follows the environmental laws and guidelines. Certain kinds of wastes (such as motor oil) are not allowed because they can seep through the earth and contaminate the soil or groundwater.

Recycling plant operator. Recycling is required by law in many cities. In other areas, concerned students have set up school and neighborhood recycling programs. Newspapers, aluminum cans, plastic items, and many types of industrial waste are taken to recycling plants, where they are converted to usable materials.

Incinerator Operator. Materials that are not recycled or buried in a landfill can be burned in large incinerators. Even some hazardous wastes can be burned. Some cities have no more room in landfills and are building waste-to-energy incinerators that burn the solid waste and use the heat to produce energy. The incinerator operator must run the facility within the environmental regulations: air and water quality standards and regulations on noise limitations and dust control.

Just about every environmental program requires taking samples of air, water, soils, or waste products to be examined for pollutants. When pollutants are identified, plans can be developed to remove them or lessen their damage to the environment. The analysis of the samples is done in an environmental laboratory by **laboratory technicians** supervised by laboratory scientists. The technicians prepare the samples for testing and then work with complicated equipment and procedures to measure the pollutants and record the test results. Although most of their work is done in the laboratory, the technician may go to a project site to take the samples.

Engineering Technicians

Engineering companies are hired to design environmentally safe buildings and projects,

Administrative jobs are also available in a recycling plant.

treatment plants, recycling centers, and hazardous-waste disposal sites. Engineering technicians may do mathematical calculations to determine pipe sizes or water pressure required; measure the types and amounts of materials needed for designs; draft designs on a computer, or collect and analyze technical information on pollution control and waste treatment equipment. A specialized engineering technician is trained to do computer-assisted design (CAD), which helps engineers rapidly prepare, alter, and finalize detailed engineering drawings.

Land surveyors are often used on large environmental projects such as construction of a hazardous-waste disposal site. Surveyors plot the layout of the site and verify the property boundaries and land elevations. Technicians assist in this work by using a transit to take measurements and plot them on engineering drawings and maps. Often, with experience and skill, technicans become certified as surveyors.

Hazardous material transporter, hazardous waste site worker, and **emergency responder** are three dangerous environmental jobs. Working with hazardous materials such as toxic chemicals or radioactive waste requires specialized training in handling the materials and in personal protection from exposure. These materials are moved by truck, plane, ship, or train and must be carefully packed and transported to reduce the danger of accidents or leaks.

Hazardous-waste technicians may work at cleanup sites or at a treatment, storage, or disposal facility. They must be fully trained in handling hazardous waste. They may have to wear special chemical resistant suits that look like a spaceman outfit. Some jobs require use of special tools to find and remove buried steel drums or underground storage tanks filled with hazardous materials.

If a hazardous waste or chemical spill occurs, emergency responders rush to the scene. They are experts in containing spills and cleaning the area as well as in protecting themselves and people in the area of the accident.

Environmental technicians are hired by a wide variety of employers including government agencies, engineering and design firms, private industry, and environmental consulting firms. Starting salaries for natural resource management and environmental technicians are in the $25,000–$35,000 range, with supervisory positions around $50,000.

Environmental Careers with College

Many environmental positions require a college degree and some require an advanced degree. This section describes many of those jobs and what they involve.

Many businesses have begun recycling programs.

The three important ingredients of the environment are the earth, the water, and the air. As seen in Chapter 1, all three are connected. If you damage one, the others are also harmed. Keep in mind as you read these brief job descriptions that each job contributes to making the earth a safer place to live.

Air Quality Engineer. The main responsibility of these engineers is to develop ways to control air pollution and follow the requirements of the Clean Air Act. Air quality engineers developed smokestack scrubbers that remove soot and other air pollutants from factory smokestack

27

emissions. They work to remove air pollutants from automobile exhausts and reduce sulfur dioxide and nitrous oxide emissions.

National Park Service Employee. Many different types of jobs are available in the National Park Service, but the overall goal is the same: to protect and preserve the parks. The law enforcement ranger protects park visitors, natural resources, and property. Maintenance workers build park roads and structures and keep the park running. Natural resource managers work to keep the vegetation, wildlife, and other resources healthy. Interpreters, who are part teachers and part tour guides, present information about the park. State and local park employees have similar jobs, but the parks are usually not as large as national parks.

Forester. These workers care for the health of the forest both by harvesting trees and by planting new trees. They also fight fires and protect the trees from disease. Foresters plan their harvesting cuts to protect the soils, wildlife, and nearby waterways.

Lobbyist. The environmental lobbyist tries to influence politicians to pass laws that will help the environment. Many environmental organizations employ a lobbyist to meet with legislators and show them the benefit of laws to protect the environment. This lobbyist must work hard and know the facts about the environment, because private industries also have lobbyists trying to influence the legislators to vote the opposite way.

Environmental Activist. This is a general term for someone who works for an environmental organization. Such organizations are numerous, and most of them specialize in one aspect of the environment. For example, the Wilderness Society wants more public lands classified as wilderness areas without roads or developments. American Rivers works to prevent the damming of free-flowing rivers. Friends of the Earth works to defeat any proposed laws that would be harmful to the earth. Most of these organizations support each other's goals. Much of their work is with local groups to improve environmental conditions and with legislators to support beneficial environmental laws.

Hazardous Materials Specialist. This highly trained expert is responsible for the use, transport, and disposal of hazardous materials such as radioactive waste. Workers are taught how to pack and transport materials and what to do if there is a leak or spill. They are also shown how to protect themselves from exposure to the materials.

Industrial Hygienist. The industrial hygienist examines daily activities in the workplace, looking for potential risks to employees. He or she also develops instructions for employees who work

The vice-president of a recycling plant stands on 25 feet of old newspaper.

Recycling helps, but it doesn't altogether solve the problem of too much waste.

with dangerous situations or materials such as removing asbestos from a building or cleaning up an oil spill. A similar job is that of Safety Engineer.

Lawyer. Because of the many environmental laws and regulations, some lawyers now specialize in environmental law. They may work for the government and help write the guidelines for businesses. They may also work for private companies and advise managers and employees on how to obey the laws. Environmental lawyers may work for law firms or be in private practice.

Environmental Engineer. These specialists analyze environmental problems and design solutions. Their activities include wastewater treatment, hazardous-waste disposal, environmentally safe landfill design, and treatment of contaminated soils and groundwater.

Noise Control Specialist. Noise control specialists develop methods of reducing noise so that it does not damage our hearing. You may have seen the noise barriers built along many expressways that run through residential areas. Noise control specialists also work with airports and heavy industries such as steel mills to reduce noise levels.

Agronomist. Traditionally, agronomists have worked to develop ways of planting, raising, and harvesting food. With the new concern for the environment, more farmers are looking at low-input agriculture, which reduces the use of fertilizers, pesticides, and harmful plowing patterns. As demand grows for environmentally clean fruits and vegetables grown without fertilizers and pesticides, more farmers are looking to agronomists for advice.

Environmental Toxicologist. This scientist evaluates the effects of hazardous chemicals on human health and the environment. Toxicologists are involved in soil and groundwater cleanup.

They measure the level of toxic materials and determine when the soil and groundwater are clean enough to be safe for human use.

Geologist. Geologists study the earth and how it has changed over millions of years. They study the rock foundations before dams, bridges, and large buildings are constructed to make sure that the foundations are strong enough to support the structures. They also help to find oil deposits in the earth. Geologists also study earthquakes, hoping to learn to predict them.

Planner. The majority of planners work for state or local governments. Planners gather information about current public and private land uses. They compare these land uses to the future goals of the government and try to develop plans for reaching those goals. They are familiar with zoning regulations and may recommend changing or creating a regulation to prevent overdevelopment near a park area or to preserve a historic landmark.

Writer. Many major newspapers have full-time environmental writers. A number of environmental magazines are published. Another option is technical writing for a government agency or private industry. Working with experts in geology, land-use planning, fisheries and wildlife, and engineering, a technical writer may write an environmental impact statement. Such a statement explains the environmental impact of a

Geologists study rocks for clues about the earth's past.

large construction project such as a hazardous-waste disposal facility or a water supply dam. They also specify what the builder intends to do to lessen the impact on the environment.

Water Quality Engineer. The water quality engineer develops ways to purify contaminated water so that it can be reused and does not harm the environment.

Environmental Protection Agency (EPA). This federal agency is charged with writing guidelines and regulations for the environmental laws. The EPA also enforces those laws. Environmental Protection Specialist is the job title for many entry-level positions with the EPA. These specialists may oversee contracts for cleaning contaminated hazardous-waste sites. They also monitor the records of manufacturers' air emissions to ensure that the quantity of pollutants released complies with the Clean Air Act. From entry-level positions, employees gain experience and can move up to managerial or policymaking positions. Most states also have an agency that enforces federal and state environmental laws.

Ecologist. Ecologists study ecosystems, which are communities of living things and their environment. The environment of an ecosystem is called a habitat. Ecologists have shown that when a habitat is destroyed, the living things that depend on it are also destroyed. To restore an endangered species, it is necessary to preserve and protect their habitat. Some ecologists do basic research and teach at universities. Others work for federal or state agencies. In their research, they try to discover how living things are connected. An ecologist may be researching which type of grass is best for stopping soil erosion, or what would happen to the birds if a swamp were to be drained. Ecology has been called the study of the balance of nature.

This chapter has given a brief sampling of some of the environmental careers. There are many specialties within some of these careers. For instance, in the field of geology are marine geologists, who study the shape and structure of the ocean floor; geochemists, who study the chemical elements in rocks and minerals; paleontologists, who are interested in the fossil remains of plants and animals that lived millions of years ago; and geophysicists, who study the earth's gravity and magnetism.

Because of the variety of careers in the environmental field, it is hard to provide a range of salaries. Jobs for which candidates are in short supply pay the highest. Engineering and hazardous waste positions average $40,000 for starting salaries and go up to $100,000 for senior management. Most of the environmental positions described pay between $20,000 and $35,000 for entry-level positions. The government generally

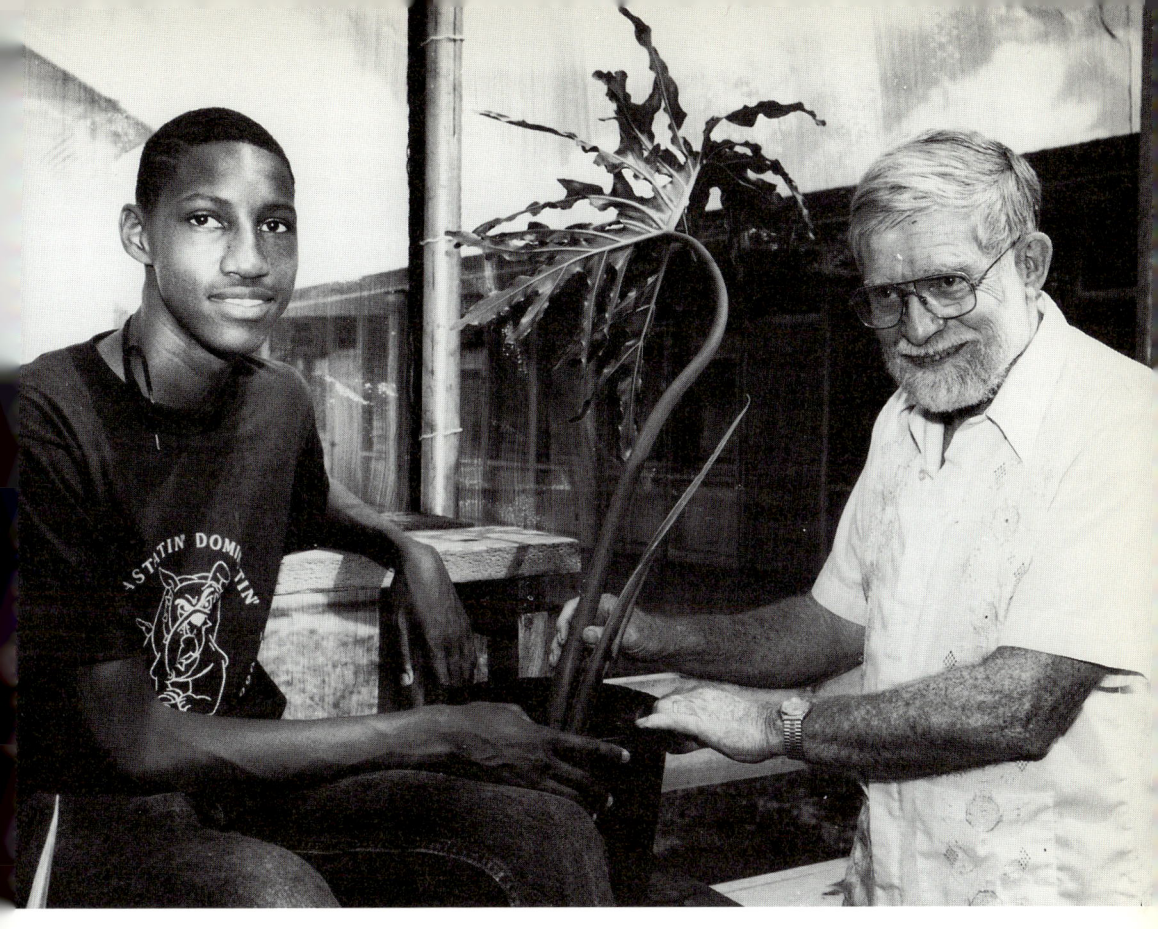

One way to learn whether or not you might enjoy a career in an environmentally related field is to work with someone who has such a job. Wesley Wilson shares his knowledge of horticulture with Fred Barnes here.

does not pay well for top management positions but pays very well for mid-level positions. Most of these are between GS-7 ($23,000) and GS-12 ($40,000). GS stands for "General Schedule," and the numbers 1 to 15 are the pay grades.

These environmental careers can be found anywhere. The work goes on across the United States. Salaries vary depending on location. They are higher in the Northeast, mid-Atlantic states, and West Coast because the cost of living is higher in these geographic areas.

Another option is to go into business for yourself. If you know where you want to live, do some intensive research in that area on the need for your job specialty. If you decide that your special talents are needed, you can consider the possibility of starting your own business. You might start a consulting firm, manufacture pollution control equipment, set up an environmental testing laboratory, or develop computer software for pollution control or natural resource programs. Whatever you decide, great risk is involved, and it may take a few years before you begin making much money.

Questions to Ask Yourself
There are many possible careers in Environmental Science. You have to decide which, if any, is the right one for you. 1) What areas of environmental science interest you? 2) What interests and skills might you need to have a successful career in environmental science? 3) Why do you want to participate in environmental sciences?

CHAPTER 4

GAINING EXPERIENCE

Employers prefer to hire people with experience. But how can you get that experience? Two ways are working part time and volunteering.

If you find a company or job that interests you, call or write the personnel office of the company and check out the possibility of part-time work. Many companies and government agencies have employment programs for students and would welcome your interest. The National Park Service and the Environmental Protection Agency employ part-time high school and college students throughout the year.

Most of these same companies and government agencies also hire students during the summer. National and state parks need help because summer is their busiest time. With schools out and families on vacation, the parks are crowded. More help is needed on the maintenance staffs

Many volunteers were needed to help clean the animals after the Exxon oil spill in Alaska in 1989.

and in the visitor centers, working with the public to ensure that they enjoy their visit.

Even if the type of work you do is not what you want as a career, part-time employment allows you to get to know the company or agency. Often students are introduced to a type of career that they had never considered. On the other hand, you may find that you are not interested in this work. It is better to know at an early stage whether or not you would enjoy a career working to improve the environment.

Part-Time Work

Brandon started a recycling program at his school. He met with the operator of the recycling plant and arranged for their truck to come to his school once a week to pick up the paper, aluminum, glass, and plastic recycling containers. With the money they receive for the recyclable materials, the student council voted to plant trees on school grounds throughout the county.

Brandon was very much interested in a career in recycling. He started to work part time at the plant, sweeping and cleaning. He asked a lot of questions about how the machines worked and who purchased the recycled materials. The operator began to move him around to different jobs to see how everything in the plant worked. Brandon was soon helping to repair machines and even run some of the machines.

When he graduated from high school, Brandon went to work full time at the recycling plant. He often goes to schools to help the students set up recycling programs, and he guides classes on tours of the plant. His goal is to be a recycling plant operator. Through his part-time job, Brandon found a career.

Volunteer

Unlike part-time workers, who are paid, volunteers donate their time. Usually volunteers are needed at national, state, and county parks and at national and local environmental organizations.

Hundreds of environmental organizations operate in the United States. Some of them focus on a single issue such as clean air or the preservation of rain forests. Others are concerned with the health of the overall environment and work against anything that will harm it.

These organizations usually have a small paid staff and depend on volunteers for help. If you want to volunteer, choose one that focuses on something that is especially interesting to you. If you are interested in wildlife, Defenders of Wildlife or the National Wildlife Federation are two such organizations.

Volunteers do a variety of jobs such as helping put the newsletter together, manning the booth at environmental fairs, fundraising, clerical work, and working with the members.

There is something for every interest among the environmental groups. The best guide is the *Conservation Directory*, published by the National Wildlife Federation. The directory contains information on thousands of national, state, and local environmental groups. It provides a short description of each group, with names, addresses, and phone numbers. It also lists and describes the federal and state government agencies.

This book is updated annually and is available in most libraries. It can also be purchased from the National Wildlife Federation, 1400 16th Street NW, Washington, DC, 20036; phone:

Appreciating the great outdoors.

(202) 797-6800. The price as of this printing was $24.55, including shipping.

The American Hiking Society publishes an annual guide, *Helping Out in the Outdoors*, listing volunteer opportunities with federal and state agencies and nonprofit organizations. Volunteers are needed to help with trail maintenance, campground management, and resource management activities. For more information, write to The American Hiking Society, 1015 31st Street NW, Washington, DC 20007.

Marisol worked as a volunteer at the Trout Unlimited national office in Vienna, Virginia. She worked two afternoons a week after school. Trout Unlimited is concerned with protecting clean water and rivers for salmon and trout. Marisol got involved because her father was a member and often took her fishing. Through her volunteer work, she became interested in a career as a fisheries biologist and plans to study for that career when she starts college.

Consider either part-time employment or volunteer work as a way of gaining valuable work experience in preparing for an environmental career. Either option may help you with your career decision.

Questions to Ask Yourself

Experience is invaluable for anyone wishing to pursue a career in environmental science. If you

If you think you want to work in the environment, you must consider how you can get the necessary experience.

think such a career is for you, you have to think about how you can get the necessary experience. 1) What are some methods of gaining work experience? 2) How can you benefit by volunteering with an environmental agency? 3) What are some agencies at which you might gain work experience?

CHAPTER 5

GETTING THE JOB

You've found the type of work you want to do. How do you go about getting a job? The direct way is to get in touch with the company or government agency you want to work for and ask them what openings are available and how to apply. Colleges have job placement centers where companies and government agencies come and interview students.

Usually you can't wait for someone to offer you a job. You must be aggressive and make the first move. Often the particular job you want is not available but another opening is. You must decide whether to take the open position, work hard and build a good reputation, and hope for the job you want to become available. If you do, your chances should be pretty good.

You are already working for the company, and you have built a good reputation. You may have the inside track for the new job.

Deon graduated with a degree in wildlife biology, but the only job available was at Great Smoky Mountains National Park (Tennessee/North Carolina) as a clerk/typist. He took the job and held it for eight months before a wildlife biologist position opened up at Everglades National Park in Florida. Since Deon was already employed by the Park Service, he had an advantage when he applied for the Everglades job.

On the other hand, you may not want to be detoured by this indirect route. In that case, keep seeking the job you want with different companies or government agencies.

One thing you need to develop is a résumé, a brief history of yourself. If you are just starting out, your résumé will probably be brief, but you should include any volunteer or part-time work experience that applies to the job you are seeking.

Many books are available at libraries on writing a résumé. Generally you should try to get your employment and educational history information on one page. Include your address and phone number, and offer to provide references if the employer requests them. Also write a cover letter to accompany the résumé.

Nicole is applying for a job as a parks and recreation technician at Yellowstone National

Park. She has just graduated from high school. Here is her résumé.

Nicole Cutrona
2242 Cedar Lane
Lansing, Michigan 67259
phone: (517) 890-3212

Experience:
- Cedar River State Park: Employed during summers 1990–1993. Checked erosion patterns, cleared hiking trails, general maintenance.
- Cedar River State Park: Employed during weekends 1989–1993 at the information desk and as a park tour guide.
- Friends of the Earth: Volunteer work 1990–1993 editing the newsletter and researching information requests from the members.
- Little Caesars Pizza: Part-time job, 1991, making pizzas.
- Sports Authority: Part-time job 1989–1990, as clerk at sporting goods store.

Education: East Lansing High School, 1989–1993. National Honor Society.

Other: Member of American Rivers and the National Parks and Conservation Association.

References: Furnished upon request.

Nicole's job with the state park shows the employer that she is familiar with the responsibilites of a parks and recreation technician. It also shows that she worked on weekends during college in a job that involved meeting the public and giving oral presentations to them. Her volunteer work with Friends of the Earth shows a commitment to the environment and her willingness to forgo a salary to help the environmental organization. The other jobs with Little Caesars and Sports Authority were held during high school and show her willingness to work.

The Education section should include any honors you received in school. The Other section is the place to put activities in organizations or societies that are relevant to the job.

Your references should be supervisors from your previous employment or volunteer work. Be sure to ask permission from these people before using their names.

You should keep your résumé updated as you acquire more skills and take on more responsibility.

When sending your résumé to a possible employer, you need to send a short cover letter to introduce yourself. Here is Nicole's cover letter.

Getting involved in activism can help your career.

Nicole Cutrona
2242 Cedar Lane
Lansing, Michigan
67259

July 15, 1994

Ms. Patricia Cole
Yellowstone Association
P.O. Box 117
Yellowstone National Park, WY 82190

Dear Ms. Cole:
Enclosed is my résumé for the position as a parks and recreation technician with Yellowstone National Park. I will be in Wyoming for the week of August 1–7 and would be glad to meet with you at your convenience to discuss my qualifications. If you have any questions or need additional information, please contact me. I look forward to hearing from you.

Sincerely,

Nicole Cutrona

    Applying for a job with the federal government is a bit more complicated. Instead of a résumé, you need to fill out Form SF 171. Instead of salary ranges, you will be concerned with GS (General Schedule) ratings to determine your pay.

Write to the Office of Personnel Management, P.O. Box 52, Washington, DC 20415, and ask for the information packet explaining how to apply for a federal government job. Also ask for a list of regional offices and Federal Job Information Centers, where job application materials and announcements are available.

You can also write to the federal agency you want to work for and inquire about current vacancies and how to apply. The agencies that provide environmental positions are listed in the *Conservation Directory*, mentioned in Chapter 4.

There is often less paperwork involved in applying for positions with state and local government agencies. Write these agencies directly to find out how to apply and what positions are available.

The following publications list environmental job openings. Check your local library for subscription information. You might split the subscription costs with one or more friends.

Earth Work (monthly)
Student Conservation Association, Inc.
P.O. Box 550
Charlestown, NH 03603
Phone: (603) 826-4301

Environmental Careers Bulletin
11693 San Vicente Boulevard
Los Angeles, CA 90049
Phone: (213) 399-3533

Environmental Opportunities (newsletter)
Box 4957
Arcata, CA 95521
Phone: (707) 839-4640

Questions to Ask Yourself
Jobs in the environmental sciences can be very competitive. It's important to have a good résumé and to be prepared for the interview. These questions might hlep you get ideas. 1) What courses could you take in high school to help you prepare for a career in environmental science? 2) What information should you include in your résumé? 3) What are some ways of job-hunting?

CHAPTER 6

CAREER TIPS

The following tips will help you land a job or advance in your career. You have to take charge of your own career. Seek out opportunities that will help you to reach your career goals.

1. Develop your speaking and writing skills. Those who can write effectively and are at ease speaking before others advance quickly.

Mark is a hazardous-waste disposal technician. His job is dangerous but what scared him more was speaking in front of citizen groups. To overcome his nervousness, Mark joined Toastmasters International, a public speaking club, where he learned speaking techniques. He now is known for his lively, informative presentations.

2. Know the current environmental laws and regulations. You should have a thorough understanding of the laws that apply to your career choice. A water quality engineer should be completely familiar with the Clean Water Act.

It is fairly easy to become computer literate today. Most schools offer the use of computers.

Hunter was selected over six other qualified applicants for a public affairs position with the Environmental Protection Agency. During the job interview, Hunter was easily able to discuss the various environmental laws and how they had affected the environment. Although the other candidates had more experience, they didn't have Hunter's knowledge of the laws.

3. Become computer literate. This is easier today with computers available in most schools. Mapmaking and engineering design are being done on computers.

Emily became skilled with computers in high

school. After graduation, she used her ability to get a job with an environmental engineering firm. Within five years, she was in charge of the Computer-Assisted Design (CAD) Division.

4. Take the initiative in seeking out career development assignments. This is part of taking charge of your career. Look for assignments that will present new challenges.

Keitha is an agronomist with the U.S. Department of Agriculture. She heard a rumor about a team of agronomists going to South America to work with the farmers in helping to preserve the rain forest. Keitha called friends in the department and verified the rumor. Then she requested an interview with the team leader and convinced him that she would be a useful member of the team. The assignment lasted two years. During that time Keitha worked hard and learned from the other team members. She received training that would help her throughout her career.

5. If your goal is to be a supervisor, learn something from each one of your supervisors. You can learn from every job you have.

Chris was promoted to wastewater-treatment plant operator before he was thirty years old. No one had ever been promoted faster. Chris had a talent for working with people, and his employees respected him. When asked the secret of his speedy promotion, Chris said that he learned to manage the plant and people from watching his former supervisors. From the good ones, he saw why they were effective and respected and how they respected their employees. From the bad ones, he learned methods to avoid.

6. Get experience by working part time or volunteering. This is discussed in Chapter 4, but it is worth repeating. Any experience will help, even if it doesn't relate to your chosen career.

José was hired for a fish and wildlife technician position with the U.S. Forest Service even though he had little experience. He had worked on construction jobs during the summers to make money and help his family. His boss told him that he was chosen because his application showed that he had always worked when he wasn't in school. The boss remarked that he'd rather hire someone who knew how to work and train him for the job.

Follow these tips and apply them to yourself in your pursuit of an environmental career.

Questions to Ask Yourself

Many skills can help you in your career in the environmental sciences. It's important for you to develop those skills now. 1) How might you improve your skills in reading, writing, and speaking? 2) How can you find out more about environmental laws? 3) What are some ways of improving your computer skills?

GLOSSARY

activist Someone who works hard for a cause or an idea.
aquatic Living or growing in water.
carbon dioxide (CO2) The most abundant gas in the atmosphere. Made up of carbon and oxygen, it is largely responsible for global warming.
contaminate To make impure or harmful.
ecosystem Community of living and nonliving things that are interconnected and depend on one another.
emission Discharge or release.
environment The world and everything in and around it—sky, earth, water, humankind, and other living things as well as everything humans have created.
extinct No longer existing.
fossil fuel Naturally occurring fuel such as coal or natural gas, formed from the remains of prehistoric organisms.
groundwater Water that has seeped beneath the

surface of the ground and is stored in porous rock.

habitat Place where an organism lives and grows naturally.

hazardous waste Solid waste that can cause illness or even death.

landfill Place where garbage is disposed of.

native Referring to plants or animals, originating in or being characteristic of a specific area.

pesticide Chemical used to kill pests (insects, mice, etc.) in homes or on crops.

pollution Substances that soil the environment.

rain forest Dense, tropical woodlands.

recycling Reuse of materials.

solid waste Garbage, yard waste, sludge from treatment facilities, and other discarded material from industrial, commercial, agricultural, and residential activities.

technician Person who is trained or skilled in the technicalities of a subject.

toxic Poisonous.

APPENDIX

American Rivers
801 Pennsylvania Avenue SE
Washington, DC 20003-2167
202-547-6900

Canadian Environmental Network
P.O. Box 1289, Station B
Ottawa, ON K1P 5R3
613-563-2078

Children of the Green Earth
Box 95219
Seattle, WA 98145

Citizens for a Safe Environment
745 Queen Street East
Toronto, DN M4M 1H3
416-462-3860

Clean Water Action
1320 18th Street NW
Washington, DC 20036
202-457-1286

The Conservation Foundation
1250 24th Street NW
Washington, DC 20037
202-293-4800

The Cousteau Society Inc.
930 West 21st Street
Norfolk, VA 23517
804-627-1144

Defenders of Wildlife
1244 19th Street NW
Washington, DC 20036
202-659-9510

Earthwatch
P.O. Box 403N
Mt. Auburn Street
Watertown, MA 02272
617-926-8200

Environmental Defense Fund, Inc.
257 Park Avenue South
New York, NY 10010
212-505-2100

**Federation of Fly
  Fishers**
P.O. Box 1088
West Yellowstone, MT
  59758
406-646-9541

Friends of the Earth
218 D Street SE
Washington, DC 20003
202-544-2600

**Greenpeace USA,
  Inc.**
1436 U Street NW
Washington, DC 20009
202-462-1177

**National Audubon
  Society**
950 Third Avenue
New York, NY 10022
212-546-9100

**National Parks and
  Conservation
  Association**
1015 31st Street NW
Washington, DC
  20007-4406
202-944-8530

**The Nature
  Conservancy**
1815 North Lynn Street
Arlington, VA 22209
703-841-5300

**Natural Resources
  Defense Council**
40 West 20th Street
New York, NY 10011
212-727-2700

**Rainforest Action
  Network**
301 Broadway
San Francisco, CA 94133
415-398-4404

Sierra Club
730 Polk Street
San Francisco, CA 94109
415-776-2211

The Wilderness Society
900 17th Street NW
Washington, DC
  20006-2596
202-833-2300

World Wildlife Fund
1250 24th Street NW
Washington, DC 20037
202-293-4800

FOR FURTHER READING

Baldwin, J., ed. *Whole Earth Ecolog*. New York: Harmony Books, 1990.

Basta, Nicholas. *Environmental Career Guide: Job Opportunities with the Earth in Mind*. New York: John Wiley & Sons, Inc., 1991.

———. *Environmental Jobs for Scientists and Engineers*. New York: John Wiley & Sons, Inc., 1992.

Berger, Melvin. *Jobs That Save Our Environment*. New York: Lothrop, Lee and Shepard Company, 1973.

DeAngelis, L., ed. *The Complete Guide to Environmental Careers*. Washington, DC: Island Press, 1989.

Gartner, Robert. *Working Together Against the Destruction of the Environment*. New York: Rosen Publishing Group, 1994.

———. *Exploring Careers in the National Parks*. New York: Rosen Publishing Group, 1993.

Warner, David J. *Environmental Careers: A Practical Guide to Opportunities in the '90s*. Chelsea, MI: Lewis Publishers Inc., 1992.

INDEX

A
activist, environmental, 6, 13, 29
agriculture, low-input, 32
agronomist, 32, 57
American Hiking Society, 44
American Rivers, 29
application, job
　Form SF 171, 52–53

C
carbon dioxide, 10
chain reaction, 10–11, 14
Clean Air Act, 10, 28, 35
Clean Water Act, 10, 56
computer-assisted design (CAD), 25, 57
Conservation Directory, 42–44, 53
cover letter, 50–52

D
Defenders of Wildlife, 42

E
ecologist, 35–36
education, 13
　four-year college, 27
　two-year college, 16
emergency responder, 25
Endangered Species Act, 17
engineer
　air quality, 27–28
　environmental, 32
　forest, 18
　water quality, 35
Environmental Protection Agency (EPA), 6, 35, 39, 56
erosion, soil, 11, 17, 36
experience, gaining, 39–46

F
firefighter, 18
Fish & Wildlife Service, U.S., 17
forester, 28
Forest Service, U.S., 58
Friends of the Earth, 29, 50

G
geochemist, 36
geographic information system (GIS), 21
geologist, 20, 33
　marine, 36
geophysicist, 36
global warming, 10
groundtruthing, 21
groundwater
　tests, 20–21, 22
　treatment, 32, 33

H
habitat studies, 17–19, 36
harvest, timber, 19–20
hazardous material specialist, 29–31
hazardous material transporter, 25–26
hazardous waste
　disposal, 20–21, 23, 25, 32, 35, 55
　site worker, 25–26
　specialist, 14

I
incinerator operator, 23
industrial hygienist, 29–31

J
job
　getting, the, 47–53
　part-time, 39–41, 58

L
landfill, sanitary, 22, 32
land surveyor, 25

63

laws, environmental, 6, 22, 29, 35, 55–56
lawyer, environmental, 32
lobbyist, 28–29

N
National Park Service, 28, 39
National Wildlife Federation, 10, 42, 48
noise control specialist, 32

P
paleontologist, 36
petitions, circulating, 9–10
planner, 33
pollution
  air, 10
  control, 25
  limiting, 6
  testing for, 14, 17, 20–21, 23, 35

R
recycling, 6, 9, 41
  plant operator, 22–23
résumé, 48–49

S
safety engineer, 31
salaries, 13, 26, 37
skills
  computer literacy, 56–57
  speaking and writing, 55
species, endangered, 9, 19, 36

T
technician
  engineering, 25–26
  environmental, 14, 16, 21–25
  fish and wildlife, 17, 58
  forestry, 18–20
  geology, 20
  hazardous waste, 36
  land-use planning, 21
  natural resource management, 16–17
  parks and recreation, 20
timber cruising, 18
tips, career, 55–59
toxicologist, environmental, 33
Trout Unlimited, 44

V
volunteering, 10, 42–45, 58

W
"walk the talk," 12–13
wastewater treatment, 21–22, 32, 57–58
Wilderness Society, 29
writer, 33–35

ABOUT THE AUTHOR
Robert Gartner spent twelve years with the National Park Service working on planning teams and natural resource programs for wild and scenic rivers, national trails, wilderness, grazing, fisheries, fire, and endangered species. He is currently a natural resource specialist for the Bureau of Indian Affairs, and lives in Burke, Virginia.

   Mr. Gartner has written articles for outdoor publications, technical journals, and newspapers. He has published two books, *The National Parks Fishing Guide* and *Careers in the National Parks*.

COVER PHOTO: © AP/Wide World
PHOTO CREDITS: © AP/Wide World
PHOTO RESEARCH: Vera Ahmadzadeh
DESIGN: Kim Sonsky